GRAB A HOLD OF YOURSELF

Pamela Denise Brown

GRAB A HOLD OF YOURSELF

ACNOWLEDGEMENT

I Would Like To Thank
My Lord And Savior

Jesus Christ

For All That God Has Given Me
I Recognize That The Lord Gave Me
This Gift
Which Allows Me To Share With
Everyone That Participates In The
Reading Of The Literary Material That I
Produce Through The Commission Of
God

Thank You Lord God

I Will Forever Be Grateful
For Your Trust In Me

Pamela Denise Brown

Books Speak For You books may be ordered through booksellers or by contacting:
Books Speak For You Educational Publishing
Booksspeakforyou.com
1-800-757-0598
The views expressed in this work are solely those of the author.
Any illustration provided by iStock and such images are being used for illustrative purposes.
Certain stock imagery © iStock.
ISBN: 978-1-64050-304-5

Library Of Congress No. 2017918675

Printed in the United States Of America

God Works His Will

Ephesians 1:11 (KJV)

[11] In whom also we have obtained an inheritance, being predestinated according to the purpose of him who worketh all things after the counsel of his own will:

God Counsels With Himself To Do His Will…

A Biblical READ…

1 Corinthians 15 King James Version

15 Moreover, brethren, I declare unto you the gospel which I preached unto you, which also ye have received, and wherein ye stand;

[2] By which also ye are saved, if ye keep in memory what I preached unto you, unless ye have believed in vain.

[3] For I delivered unto you first of all that which I also received, how that Christ died for our sins according to the scriptures;

[4] And that he was buried, and that he rose again the third day according to the scriptures:

[5] And that he was seen of Cephas, then of the twelve:

[6] After that, he was seen of above five hundred brethren at once; of whom the greater part remain unto this present, but some are fallen asleep.

[7] After that, he was seen of James; then of all the apostles.

[8] And last of all he was seen of me also, as of one born out of due time.

[9] For I am the least of the apostles, that am not meet to be called an apostle, because I persecuted the church of God.

¹⁰ But by the grace of God I am what I am: and his grace which was bestowed upon me was not in vain; but I laboured more abundantly than they all: yet not I, but the grace of God which was with me.

¹¹ Therefore whether it were I or they, so we preach, and so ye believed.

¹² Now if Christ be preached that he rose from the dead, how say some among you that there is no resurrection of the dead?

¹³ But if there be no resurrection of the dead, then is Christ not risen:

¹⁴ And if Christ be not risen, then is our preaching vain, and your faith is also vain.

¹⁵ Yea, and we are found false witnesses of God; because we have testified of God that he raised up Christ: whom he raised not up, if so be that the dead rise not.

¹⁶ For if the dead rise not, then is not Christ raised:

¹⁷ And if Christ be not raised, your faith is vain; ye are yet in your sins.

¹⁸ Then they also which are fallen asleep in Christ are perished.

¹⁹ If in this life only we have hope in Christ, we are of all men most miserable.

²⁰ But now is Christ risen from the dead, and become the firstfruits of them that slept.

²¹ For since by man came death, by man came also the resurrection of the dead.

²² For as in Adam all die, even so in Christ shall all be made alive.

²³ But every man in his own order: Christ the firstfruits; afterward they that are Christ's at his coming.

²⁴ Then cometh the end, when he shall have delivered up the kingdom to God, even the Father; when he shall have put down all rule and all authority and power.

²⁵ For he must reign, till he hath put all enemies under his feet.

²⁶ The last enemy that shall be destroyed is death.

²⁷ For he hath put all things under his feet. But when he saith all things are put under him, it is manifest that he is excepted, which did put all things under him.

²⁸ And when all things shall be subdued unto him, then shall the Son also himself be subject unto him that put all things under him, that God may be all in all.

²⁹ Else what shall they do which are baptized for the dead, if the dead rise not at all? why are they then baptized for the dead?

³⁰ And why stand we in jeopardy every hour?

³¹ I protest by your rejoicing which I have in Christ Jesus our Lord, I die daily.

³² If after the manner of men I have fought with beasts at Ephesus, what advantageth it me, if the dead rise not? let us eat and drink; for to morrow we die.

³³ Be not deceived: evil communications corrupt good manners.

³⁴ Awake to righteousness, and sin not; for some have not the knowledge of God: I speak this to your shame.

³⁵ But some man will say, How are the dead raised up? and with what body do they come?

³⁶ Thou fool, that which thou sowest is not quickened, except it die:

³⁷ And that which thou sowest, thou sowest not that body that shall be, but bare grain, it may chance of wheat, or of some other grain:

³⁸ But God giveth it a body as it hath pleased him, and to every seed his own body.

³⁹ All flesh is not the same flesh: but there is one kind of flesh of men, another flesh of beasts, another of fishes, and another of birds.

⁴⁰ There are also celestial bodies, and bodies terrestrial: but the glory of the celestial is one, and the glory of the terrestrial is another.

[41] There is one glory of the sun, and another glory of the moon, and another glory of the stars: for one star differeth from another star in glory.

[42] So also is the resurrection of the dead. It is sown in corruption; it is raised in incorruption:

[43] It is sown in dishonour; it is raised in glory: it is sown in weakness; it is raised in power:

[44] It is sown a natural body; it is raised a spiritual body. There is a natural body, and there is a spiritual body.

[45] And so it is written, The first man Adam was made a living soul; the last Adam was made a quickening spirit.

[46] Howbeit that was not first which is spiritual, but that which is natural; and afterward that which is spiritual.

[47] The first man is of the earth, earthy; the second man is the Lord from heaven.

[48] As is the earthy, such are they also that are earthy: and as is the heavenly, such are they also that are heavenly.

[49] And as we have borne the image of the earthy, we shall also bear the image of the heavenly.

[50] Now this I say, brethren, that flesh and blood cannot inherit the kingdom of God; neither doth corruption inherit incorruption.

[51] Behold, I shew you a mystery; We shall not all sleep, but we shall all be changed,

[52] In a moment, in the twinkling of an eye, at the last trump: for the trumpet shall sound, and the dead shall be raised incorruptible, and we shall be changed.

[53] For this corruptible must put on incorruption, and this mortal must put on immortality.

[54] So when this corruptible shall have put on incorruption, and this mortal shall have put on immortality, then shall be brought to pass the saying that is written, Death is swallowed up in victory.

[55] O death, where is thy sting? O grave, where is thy victory?

[56] The sting of death is sin; and the strength of sin is the law.

[57] But thanks be to God, which giveth us the victory through our Lord Jesus Christ.

[58] Therefore, my beloved brethren, be ye stedfast, unmoveable, always abounding in the work of the Lord, forasmuch as ye know that your labour is not in vain in the Lord.

Introduction To The Read

It's Tuesday, April 18, 2017, 11:09 pm I feel like there has been a rebirth and I've literally been born again. Coming to the end of who I was and walking into who I am in Christ, in God. The bible teaches us that God knew us before we were in our mother's womb and perhaps that scripture can in a nutshell explain the feeling that I am now experiencing. It's kinda more like an awakening of what has already been and I've just finally caught up with myself in the spirit of who I am in the scope of who I exist as.

The Lord is everything to me, hallelujah, everything to me and I feel unattached to myself, yet, I Am myself.

I believe that when you are realized, in truth and the truth is absolute in your existence, you can then move forward with that knowledge in the perspective that your life now is powered by the truth of the image of God you were created in.

Now, the only thing you can do is move forward in conscious knowledge that your life has literally been a lie and everything you did without the knowledge of truth was on borrowed time that you managed to escape death in and live to tell about it. There is a scripture that references the dead in Christ rising.

There are also scriptures about Jesus raising Lazurus from the dead.

I feel like a resurrection has occurred, a reincarnation of a pre-incarnation of what God called already to exist. This is the mindset that I am currently in as I am experiencing the "SWITCH" or as I described early on the "re-birth".

Nicodemus asked Jesus a question, "what must I do to enter into the kingdom" and Jesus answered, "you must be born again".

Jesus was not speaking of an actual rebirth that included the traveling through the womb, but I want to conclude that it meant coming to the realization of who God is in divine absolute mind and accepting it as your purpose in purpose, your person in person and your existence in existence. Born again, with the knowledge that the way you lived, thought, acted was all wrong, unless of course you had the mind of Christ that included knowledge of Christ, that included the renewing of your mind to include transformation with the renewed mind in truth in God through Christ. Hallelujah, this is a little overwhelming, as I sit here and now wonder how did I wound up in this place, in this seat, in this space on this earth. I feel like I am somewhere I should not be and the only way for me to "escape" and "get back home" is to journey on through the rite of passage that I have been given to get to the other side.

Is this making any sense to anyone?

Starting all over can be quite scary, especially when it has suddenly occurred without notice or explanation. It just happened, it's not like I went to sleep and woke up on the other side. I just arrived or maybe moved in time, through time, without even moving in time

October 5, 2017…

I am re-starting this book, "Grab A Hold Of Yourself" With The Hopes Of "Completing" It In 7 Days…

There Were So Many Ways, This Book Could Have Been Written…

The Title Itself Speaks Volumes And In That Comes A Command, A Directive And Instructions.

I Was Called To Write This Book, It's Funny, Because My "Close Person" Is Always Telling Me, Pamela Grab A Hold Of Yourself… I Would Just Look At Him, But I "Realized" That I Had To Grab A Hold Of Myself. I Had To Grab A Hold Of My Behavior, The Way I Acted, The Way I Responded, The Way I Spoke, How I Interacted With People And The Things I Did…

Now That We Got That Out The Way, Let's Move Forward With The Book, Which By The Way I Started Again, October 29, 2017 After This Paragraph.

At Some Point, You Have To Grab A Hold Of Yourself. This Is Important, Because You Cannot Be Successful, Productive Or Advance In Christ If You Have No Self Control, There Are Just Some Things You Just Can't Do Anymore. There Comes A Time In Everybody's Life When You Really Just Have To Face Exactly Who You Are, Who You're Not And Who You Really Want To Be. You Can Not Move Forward In Life Or In Christ And Never Confront Yourself, It's Just Not Possible. Your Life Is Going To Run Into A Wall At Some Point And You Will Begin To Ask Questions Regarding What's Going On In Your Life And More Importantly, What's Not Going On.

Trust Me, When You Really Desire To Live Holy, The Word Of God In You Will Start Correcting You…

God's Word Is SURE…

The Bible Says… Psalm 119:11 (KJV)

[11] Thy word have I hid in mine heart, that I might not sin against thee.

Believe Me, I Know…

You Will Eventually Be Called To Your Created, Corrected Self. (It's Marvelous) AND The Journey Is Real!!!

Mind…

There's A Scripture In The Bible That Says In Philippians 2:5 ^{5} Let this mind be in you, which was also in Christ Jesus: But What Actually Does That Mean? Let Me Add Most Of The 2nd Chapter That We May Get The "Full" Understanding Of What That Means And Then I'll Go Back Into Grabbing A Hold Of Your Mind, Following This Biblical Precept.

Philippians 2 King James Version

2 If there be therefore any consolation in Christ, if any comfort of love, if any fellowship of the Spirit, if any bowels and mercies,

^{2} Fulfil ye my joy, that ye be likeminded, having the same love, being of one accord, of one mind.

^{3} Let nothing be done through strife or vainglory; but in lowliness of mind let each esteem other better than themselves.

^{4} Look not every man on his own things, but every man also on the things of others.

^{5} Let this mind be in you, which was also in Christ Jesus:

^{6} Who, being in the form of God, thought it not robbery to be equal with God:

[7] But made himself of no reputation, and took upon him the form of a servant, and was made in the likeness of men:

[8] And being found in fashion as a man, he humbled himself, and became obedient unto death, even the death of the cross.

[9] Wherefore God also hath highly exalted him, and given him a name which is above every name:

[10] That at the name of Jesus every knee should bow, of things in heaven, and things in earth, and things under the earth;

[11] And that every tongue should confess that Jesus Christ is Lord, to the glory of God the Father.

[12] Wherefore, my beloved, as ye have always obeyed, not as in my presence only, but now much more in my absence, work out your own salvation with fear and trembling.

[13] For it is God which worketh in you both to will and to do of his good pleasure.

[14] Do all things without murmurings and disputings:

[15] That ye may be blameless and harmless, the sons of God, without rebuke, in the midst of a crooked and perverse nation, among whom ye shine as lights in the world;

[16] Holding forth the word of life; that I may rejoice in the day of Christ, that I have not run in vain, neither laboured in vain.

[17] Yea, and if I be offered upon the sacrifice and service of your faith, I joy, and rejoice with you all.

[18] For the same cause also do ye joy, and rejoice with me.

[19] But I trust in the Lord Jesus to send Timotheus shortly unto you, that I also may be of good comfort, when I know your state.

[20] For I have no man likeminded, who will naturally care for your state.

[21] For all seek their own, not the things which are Jesus Christ's.

When I Say, Grab A Hold Of Your Mind, I Am Saying In A Nut Shell, Grab A Hold Of The Way You Think, So What You Say Will "Reflect" The Like Mind Of Christ.

If We Don't Have The Mind Of Christ, We Walk After Our Flesh Minds And In Those Thoughts, We Could Be Praying One Minute And Cursing Someone Out In The Next. Grabbing A Hold Of Your Mind Constantly Is To Always Be Aware Of "Who You Are", "Who You Represent", "Who You Belong To", With The

Understanding That You Are Being Watched By God And Being Held "Accountable To What You Do And What You Say And Also How What You Do And Say "Affects" Other People.

There Is A Scripture That Actually Helped Me To "Grab A Hold Of My Mind" As It Related To What I Said And That Scripture Is "Now" Always Before Me In Thought Before I Say Things, Because God Dropped It In My Spirit As a "Reminder", That I Would 1. Not Sin,

2. Not Offend Anyone

And

3.Be Held Accountable For My Actions And Ultimately "Realize" What My Outcome For It Would Be.

The Scripture That "Sits" In My Head And Gives Me "Fear" To Be Obedient Is This And Guys, If You Are Trying To Live Right And Pleasing In The Sight Of God... This Will Check You...

The Bible Says This... And Wait

Before I Give It To You... It's In The Bible 3 Times... So You Know, God Is Serious, Because Matthew, Mark And Luke Say It...

Matthew 18:6King James Version (KJV)

[6] But whoso shall offend one of these little ones which believe in me, it were better for him that a millstone were hanged about his neck, and that he were drowned in the depth of the sea.

Mark 9:42King James Version (KJV)

[42] And whosoever shall offend one of these little ones that believe in me, it is better for him that a millstone were hanged about his neck, and he were cast into the sea.

Luke 17:2King James Version (KJV)

[2] It were better for him that a millstone were hanged about his neck, and he cast into the sea, than that he should offend one of these little ones.

God Is Not Playing With Us...

We Need To Get Ourselves Together And Get It Right...

God Has Made A Way Of Escape For Us And The Bible Says... Thy Word Have I Hid In My Heart, That I Might Not Sin Against Thee.

I Believe That We Should Begin To Look Up All The Scriptures That Are Geared To Correct Us.

We Are So Familiar With Scriptures and Verses That Promise Us A Reward...

That Talk About The Goodness Of God…

That Tell Us If We Do Right We'll Be Blessed, But I Challenge You This Day To Pull Out The Scriptures That Check You, That Tell You If You Don't Keep God's Commandments You're Going To Hell, That Tell You If You Offend Someone You'll Pay, That Tell You The Wages Of Sin Is Death…

The Scriptures That "Scare You", Give You A Conscious And Make You Want To Do Right, Act Right, Walk Right, Talk Right, Live Right, Treat Other People Right…

You Know The Nitti Gritty Scriptures That Make You Want To Be "Christ Like"…

The Bible Says That God Winks At Our Ignorance,
SEE: Acts 17:30-31 (KJV)

[30] And the times of this ignorance God winked at; but now commandeth all men every where to repent:

[31] Because he hath appointed a day, in the which he will judge the world in righteousness by that man whom he hath ordained; whereof he hath given assurance unto all men, in that he hath raised him from the dead.

When You Know Better, You Should Want To Do Better And Be Better.

The Bible Says Be Ye Holy, For I Am Holy.

Let Me Get That For You, Because Surprisingly, The Bible Does Not Say, Practice On Being Holy, Try To Be Holy, Work On Being Holy, It Says…. And If You Have An Imagination, Imagine Me With A Bull Horn

Saying *"BE YE HOLY"…*

1 Peter 1:15-17 King James Version

[15] But as he which hath called you is holy, so be ye holy in all manner of conversation;

[16] Because it is written, Be ye holy; for I am holy.

God Is Calling Us To Holiness…

Righteousness…

Calling Us To Be Like Him…

Calling Us To Esteem Not Ourselves But Others…

Calling Us To Love Unconditionally…

Calling Us Not To Do Things That We May Be Glorified…

Calling Us To Do His Good Pleasure…

Calling Us That We May Be Blameless And Harmless…

Calling Us That We May Be A Representation Of Light Through Christ…

We Are Being Called To The "High" Calling And The Only Way To Get There Is To "Grab A Hold Of Yourself" And Let The Transformation Begin With The Word Of God…

We Are More And I'll Say It Again, We Are More Than Conquerors…

So I'm Now Asking You, Is There Anything Too Hard For God???

God Is Able To Keep Us From Falling…

We Are Pressing Toward The High Calling As We Journey Through The Wilderness Of Life…

Remembering Of Course Like I Often Say In My Post…

Acts 17:28 King James Version

[28] For in him we live, and move, and have our being; as certain also of your own poets have said, For we are also his offspring.

We Live And Move And Have Our Being In Him And We Must "Grab A Hold Of Ourselves" That We May Walk Upright And Have The Mind Of Christ…

God Is Indeed Good To Us..

God Breathed Into Us…

God Sent His Son To Die For Us…

Now We Must Grab A Hold Of Ourselves, Because In Actuality We Owe God Our Lives And When We Can Grab A Hold Of That Knowledge In Retrospect, We Can Grab A Hold Of Ourselves.

How You Think, What You Do, How You Do It And What You Say…

Now That I Got That Out The Way, I'm Going To Talk About Grabbing A Hold Of The Way You Think, What You Do, How You Do It, How You Interact With People And What You Say…

All Of This Of Course Is Continued In The Word Of God, In God's Directive For Your Life That You May Be Who God Created And Called You To Be…

You Do Understand The "Press For The High Calling" Right???

Philippians 3:14 (kjv) [14] I press toward the mark for the prize of the high calling of God in Christ Jesus.

The Bible Teaches Us This And This Is A "Teachable Moment", So Let's "Define"

Press…

Mark…

Prize…

High…

AND Calling Just To Be CLEAR…

Press: transitive verb 1: to act upon through steady pushing or thrusting force exerted in contact.

Mark: Target (a goal to be achieved)

Prize: something highly valuable, something unusually valuable or eagerly sought, something exceptionally desirable.

High: situated or passing above normal level, surface, or elevation

Calling: a strong urge toward a particular way of life.

So In Essence God Is Calling Us The Steadily Push Toward Him In Like, Which Is The Mark Toward The Prize, Which Is In Heaven By Way Of How We Live And As Such We Should Set A High Standard Of Living For Ourselves That We May Answer The Call And Live A Holy Life.

The High Calling Of God Is The Divine Summons Extended To The Believer For Salvation.

Don't Get Scared, All Of This Is In Line With "Grabbing A Hold Of Yourself" And I Am, Running Forward With It That You May Hop On This Train And Benefit From The Ride!

The Ride Of Your Life!!!

How You Think:

Now Let's Get To How You Think…

I Believe I Covered That In Debt, But I Will Briefly Give It To You Another Way And Really It's Simple, We Need To Just Think Like Christ. What I'm Simply Saying Is That We Should Have A Conversation With Ourselves And Ask Ourselves, What Would Christ Do? How Would Christ Think? And What Would Christ Say?...

I Believe That If We Changed The Way We Think, Life Would Be 100% Better.

Trust Me, I Am Speaking To You From My Heart, Change Sometimes Is Difficult. We Have Layers Of Life Laid On Us And Honestly, We Have To Scrape Off The Residue Of Our Life Before Christ Daily.

What You Do:

When I Say This, As I Said Earlier, We Should Be Careful Not To Offend People, Not To Hurt People And Not Cause People To Fall. We Should Be Careful Not To Lie, Not To Commit Fornication Or Commit Any Offense Toward God, That God Considers Sin.

Our Pursuit Should Be To Figure Out What God Hates And NOT Do It.

There Is A Scriptures In The Bible That Says…

Psalm 1 King James Version

1 Blessed is the man that walketh not in the counsel of the ungodly, nor standeth in the way of sinners, nor sitteth in the seat of the scornful.

2 But his delight is in the law of the LORD; and in his law doth he meditate day and night.

I Want To "Concentrate" On "Standeth In The Way Of Sinners, Nor Sitteth In The Seat Of The Scornful."

Let's Talk About This Scripture… The Bible Says "Blessed" Is The Man That *"Walketh NOT"* In The Counsel Of The Ungodly…

The Counsel Of The Ungodly Is Ungodly Advice That Comes From Ungodly People.,.

In Addition To That, *"The counsel of the ungodly"* Also *refers to advice that encourages people to live evil lives without concern for righteousness or obedience to God* (quoted from bible net)

Any Advice That Is "Contrary To God's Word Is "Ungodly", Like Divorce, Abortion Or People Giving You Advice That Causes You To Lie, Steal Or Cheat... Listen, This May Be Simple And A Lot Of People Do This Without Thought, But A Lie Is A Lie And I Am "Simplistically" Giving You A Scenario Involving A Lie. You May Think Is "Innocent" And Unnoticed, But God Sees All And He, Judges In Righteousness By What He Considers Righteousness And NOT What We Consider To Be OK Or As Some Of Us Say, "A Fib"...

Look At This Scenario: You've Been On Your Job For 3 Years And You've Never Used Sick Time. The Company Has A Policy That All Sick Time Must Be Taken By The Year End. Your Running Out Of Time And You've Accumulated 200 Sick Hours And You Still Have 7 Weeks Of Vacation Time. Your Manager Informs You That You're Going To Lose The Time And Encourages You To Make Up A Lie To Get Your Sick Time. You Agree To Do This Instead Of Taking The

Loss And Next Time, Utilizing The Time Within The Time Frame The Company Gave You To Take It.

This Is Not Only A Lie, But It's Also Walking In The Counsel Of The Ungodly And Some Of You Do It Without Thought.

It Seems Like A Small Thing In The "Natural", But To Lie Is To Sin And God's Word Clearly Says…

1 Corinthians 6:9-11 King James Version

[9] Know ye not that the **unrighteous shall not inherit the kingdom of God**? **Be not deceived**: neither fornicators, nor idolaters, nor adulterers, nor effeminate, nor abusers of themselves with mankind,

[10] Nor thieves, nor covetous, nor drunkards, nor revilers, nor extortioners, shall inherit the kingdom of God.

GOD IS NOT PLAYING WITH US…

LOOK What Revelation Says…

So For All Of Us, Including Me That Think You Can Keep Lying, Fornicating And Doing What You're Doing,

Please Read This Scripture…

And After You Read It…

"Grab A Hold Of Yourself" And Ask God To Lead You, Guide You, But More Importantly Repent AND Turn From Your Old Ways…

Look At Revelations:

Revelation 21-22King James Version

21 And I saw a new heaven and a new earth: for the first heaven and the first earth were passed away; and there was no more sea.

[2] And I John saw the holy city, new Jerusalem, coming down from God out of heaven, prepared as a bride adorned for her husband.

[3] And I heard a great voice out of heaven saying, Behold, the tabernacle of God is with men, and he will dwell with them, and they shall be his people, and God himself shall be with them, and be their God.

[4] And God shall wipe away all tears from their eyes; and there shall be no more death, neither sorrow, nor crying, neither shall there be any more pain: *for the former things are passed away.*

⁵ And he that sat upon the throne said, Behold, I make all things new. And he said unto me, **Write: for these words are true and faithful.**

⁶ And he said unto me, It is done. I am Alpha and Omega, the beginning and the end. I will give unto him that is athirst of the fountain of the water of life freely.

⁷ *He that overcometh shall inherit all things; and I will be his God, and he shall be my son.*

⁸ But the fearful, and unbelieving, and the abominable, and murderers, and whoremongers, and sorcerers, and idolaters, **and all liars**, shall have their part in the lake which burneth with fire and brimstone: which is the second death.

Now, I Really, Really Believe That It's Time For Us To Start Finding Out WHAT GOD DOES NOT LIKE And What God Does Not Want Us To Do…

I Personally Believe Jesus Is On His Way Back…

I "Don't" Care What Anyone Else Thinks Concerning This Matter. It Is My Belief And I Stand By God's Word In What He Hates And What He Likes…

I Stand By God's "Requirements" For Our Lives And His Directives As It Relates To Living A Holy Life, Hence, Grabbing A Hold Of Ourselves…

Grabbing A Hold Of Our Minds…

How We Think…

What We Think…

What We Do…

How We Do It…

What We Say…

How We Say It…

Who We Offend…

And So On, And So On…

It's Time To Live Holy…

Party #OVER!!!

There Are A Number Of Scriptures That Help Us Or I'll Say That Give Us Examples As To How We Should Act And It's Up To Us To Discover Them By Searching Them Out.

We Must Want For Others What We Want For Ourselves In Christ.

We Must See Salvation For Others The Way We See It For Ourselves.

We Must Not Want Others To Perish Just As God Doesn't Want Us To Perish.

SEE 2 Peter 3:9 King James Version

[9] The Lord is not slack concerning his promise, as some men count slackness; but is longsuffering to us-ward, **not willing that any should perish**, but that all should come to repentance.

All Of This Involves **"Grabbing A Hold Of Yourself"**.

How You Do It:

In Grabbing A Hold Of Yourself, I Am Going To Take This To Another Level, A Level Of Holiness And I Am Going To Pull A Scripture Out Of The Old Testament And Set The Bar "HIGH" So You Can Have For One, Something To Reach For And Two, A Clear Understanding From Another View On How You Reach This Goal.

I Want To Also Add Before I Bring It To You That It Be "Realized" Through The Eyes Of Love.

What Do You Mean Pamela…
I'm Glad You Asked (lol) And I Am Laughing, Enjoying My Conversation With You!!!

So, When I Say It Must Be Realized Through The Eyes Of Love, I Am Saying That Doing Anything For Anybody Is "Easier" When You Love Them. A Husband Will Do Anything For His Wife When He Loves Her And Likewise So Will A Wife.
Partners In Love Make Sacrifices For Each Other Again, Because Of Love And This Is Why I Said,

It Must Be "Realized" Through The Eyes Of Love So You Won't Think Of It As A Chore…

So Here Are The Scriptures And They're Good…

This For Sure Is A Press Toward A Call That's High!

Keep In Line This Is In Conjunction With What You Should Do In The Pursuit To "Grabbing A Hold Of Yourself".

Matthew 22:37-39
King James Version

[37] Jesus said unto him, Thou shalt love the Lord thy God with all thy heart, and with all thy soul, and with all thy mind.

[38] This is the first and great commandment.

[39] And the second is like unto it, Thou shalt love thy neighbour as thyself.

Now In Retrospect To How To Grab A Hold Of Yourself, You Do It By Doing The Will Of God In Totality Of The Whole Book…

The Instruction Of The Word In Totality…

The Instruction Of The Word In Deed…

To Do It…
Be It…
Become It...
Because, The "Ultimate" Goal Here Is To "Grab A Hold Of Yourself" That You May Live A Better Life, Have A Better Life And Become Who God Wants You To Become.

We Are Created To Serve God…
We Are Created To Bring God Glory…
We Are Created To Worship God…
PERIOD…

Jerimiah 6: 16 Says *Jeremiah 6:16King James Version (KJV)*
[16] *Thus saith the LORD, Stand ye in the ways, and see, and ask for the old paths, where is the good way, and walk therein, and ye shall find rest for your souls. But they said, We will not walk therein.*

I Know That Was A Bit Much…

I'm Really Talking About Having A "Relationship" With God Period.

You Must Be In A Relationship With God In Order To "Grab A Hold Of Yourself", Because In It, The Relationship That Is, You Correct Yourself.

God Calls You To A Place In Him And In That Place, You Correct Yourself With The Word Of God That's In You…

I'm Right Now Reminded Of A Scripture That Says…

Psalm 119:11 King James Version

[11] *Thy word have I hid in mine heart, that I might not sin against thee.*

HEAR ME CLEAR…

Grab A Hold Of Your Mind, Your Thoughts, How You Think, What You Think, What You Do And How You Do It…

When You Do That With God's Word… It Will Accomplish What It Is Suppose To Accomplish.

Again, The Scripture Says, Thy Word Have I Hid In My Heart, That I Might Not Sin Against Thee…

In Other Words, If You Hide God's Word In Your Heart, You Are Not Likely To Sin Against Him…

Key Words… "Hid In My Heart", Another Example Of What To Do.

I'm Going To Take A Stroll With You, Wrap My Arms Around You And Embrace You Slowly With The Word Of God, That It May Take Root In You And Fall On Good Ground That You May Make Up Your Mind To Do It.

Please Read This, It Is First Instructing Us To Be Followers Of God As Dear Children And To Secondly Walk In Love. This I Promise Will Not Be A Chore, Once You "Grab A Hold Of Yourself" And Begin To See Yourself First As A Sinner REALLY Saved By Grace. You Must Walk The Grateful Walk, So You Can Clearly SEE What God Has Really Done For You And For Me.

Ephesians 5 King James Version

5 Be ye therefore followers of God, as dear children;
2 And walk in love, as Christ also hath loved us, and hath given himself for us an offering and a sacrifice to God for a sweet smelling savour.

³ But fornication, and all uncleanness, or covetousness, let it not be once named among you, as becometh saints;

⁴ Neither filthiness, nor foolish talking, nor jesting, which are not convenient: but rather giving of thanks.

⁵ For this ye know, that no whoremonger, nor unclean person, nor covetous man, who is an idolater, hath any inheritance in the kingdom of Christ and of God.

⁶ Let no man deceive you with vain words: for because of these things cometh the wrath of God upon the children of disobedience.

⁷ Be not ye therefore partakers with them.

⁸ For ye were sometimes darkness, but now are ye light in the Lord: walk as children of light:

⁹ (For the fruit of the Spirit is in all goodness and righteousness and truth;)

¹⁰ Proving what is acceptable unto the Lord.

¹¹ And have no fellowship with the unfruitful works of darkness, but rather reprove them.

¹² For it is a shame even to speak of those things which are done of them in secret.

¹³ But all things that are reproved are made manifest by the light: for whatsoever doth make manifest is light.

¹⁴ Wherefore he saith, Awake thou that sleepest, and arise from the dead, and Christ shall give thee light.

¹⁵ See then that ye walk circumspectly, not as fools, but as wise,

¹⁶ Redeeming the time, because the days are evil.

¹⁷ Wherefore be ye not unwise, but understanding what the will of the Lord is.

¹⁸ And be not drunk with wine, wherein is excess; but be filled with the Spirit;

¹⁹ Speaking to yourselves in psalms and hymns and spiritual songs, singing and making melody in your heart to the Lord;

²⁰ Giving thanks always for all things unto God and the Father in the name of our Lord Jesus Christ;

²¹ Submitting yourselves one to another in the fear of God.

²² Wives, submit yourselves unto your own husbands, as unto the Lord.

²³ For the husband is the head of the wife, even as Christ is the head of the church: and he is the saviour of the body.

²⁴ Therefore as the church is subject unto Christ, so let the wives be to their own husbands in every thing.

²⁵ Husbands, love your wives, even as Christ also loved the church, and gave himself for it;

²⁶ That he might sanctify and cleanse it with the washing of water by the word,

²⁷ That he might present it to himself a glorious church, not having spot, or wrinkle, or any such thing; but that it should be holy and without blemish.

²⁸ So ought men to love their wives as their own bodies. He that loveth his wife loveth himself.

²⁹ For no man ever yet hated his own flesh; but nourisheth and cherisheth it, even as the Lord the church:

³⁰ For we are members of his body, of his flesh, and of his bones.

³¹ For this cause shall a man leave his father and mother, and shall be joined unto his wife, and they two shall be one flesh.

³² This is a great mystery: but I speak concerning Christ and the church.

³³ Nevertheless let every one of you in particular so love his wife even as himself; and the wife see that she reverence her husband.

What You Say

This Right Here Is The "Ultimate" In "Grabbing A Hold Of Yourself".

I Work On This "Daily"…

I Have So Many "Holes" In My Tongue From The Past…

(laughing out loud)

AND

I AM, Laughing Out Loud…

I Grabbed A Hold Of My Tongue By This One Scripture And Let Me Tell You, It RINGS Daily In My Ear.

There Are A Lot Of Scriptures That Help Us Grab A Hold Of Ourselves In What We Say, I'll Give You The One That "Seized My Tongue" AND Put It Under "Arrest"… (laughing again, I Am out loud)

The Scripture Is Clear, It Needs No Interpretation And Let Me Just Say This, If You Can Continue To Say Offensive Things To People Without Regards To How You Effect Them, I Am Praying For You. This Scripture Checked Me Immediately And EVERY TIME I Think About Saying Something To Someone That's Crazy, Or Off Track, Whether They Deserve It Or Not, This

Scripture Is Written On The Forefront Of My Mind And
I Am Immediately, Immediately Withdrawn.

Enough Of The Delay, Lets Get It!!!
It's Written In Matthew, Mark And John…
I Need Not Break It Down…
#Bullseye!!!

Matthew 18:6King James Version (KJV)

⁶ But whoso shall offend one of these little ones which believe in me, it were better for him that a millstone were hanged about his neck, and that he were drowned in the depth of the sea.

Mark 9:42King James Version (KJV)

⁴² And whosoever shall offend one of these little ones that believe in me, it is better for him that a millstone were hanged about his neck, and he were cast into the sea.

Luke 17:2King James Version (KJV)

² It were better for him that a millstone were hanged about his neck, and he cast into the sea, than that he should offend one of these little ones.

You Can Play Games With Yourself On This One…
I'm Good…
I Got The Message…
I Understand The Consequences…

The Price Is Too High To Pay For Disobedience, So I Beseech, Employ, Entreat, Implore, Beg, Ask, Request And Petition You Brethren To Obey The Will Of God.

Reminding You That The Wages Of Sin Is Death And Disobedience Is Sin To God.

Oh… You Don't Believe Me Or Do You Question That Disobedience Is Sin To God.

Well Since You Are Walking In The Light With Pamela", Let Me Get You Scripture.

1 Samuel 15:23 King James Version
23 *For rebellion is as the sin of witchcraft, and stubbornness is as iniquity and idolatry. Because thou hast rejected the word of the LORD, he hath also rejected thee from being king.*

Therefore, As You Continue To "Grab A Hold Of Yourself" And To Live A Holy Life, Make Sure You Grab A Hold Of Your Mouth…

Here Are Some Additional Scriptures That Can Help You Develop.

James 3:10King James Version (KJV)

[10] Out of the same mouth proceedeth blessing and cursing. My brethren, these things ought not so to be.

Proverbs 16King James Version (KJV)

16 The preparations of the heart in man, and the answer of the tongue, is from the LORD.

[2] All the ways of a man are clean in his own eyes; but the LORD weigheth the spirits.

[3] Commit thy works unto the LORD, and thy thoughts shall be established.

[4] The LORD hath made all things for himself: yea, even the wicked for the day of evil.

[5] Every one that is proud in heart is an abomination to the LORD: though hand join in hand, he shall not be unpunished.

[6] By mercy and truth iniquity is purged: and by the fear of the LORD men depart from evil.

[7] When a man's ways please the LORD, he maketh even his enemies to be at peace with him.

[8] Better is a little with righteousness than great revenues without right.

[9] A man's heart deviseth his way: but the LORD directeth his steps.

Everybody Wants To "Benefit" From Being A Christian In Word, Everybody Wants To Gain The Benefits Of God, The Promises, The Blessings, The Provision And Gods Love, But What Are We Willing To Do For It.

God Is A Covenant Making God.

God Is A God Of Rules, Standards And Laws.

The Kingdom Of God Is About Righteousness.

The Bible Directs Us To Seek The Kingdom Of God And It's Righteousness And It Clearly States After That, Everything Else Will Be "Added"... Key Word Here "Added", Which Means, You Won't Have To Ask, God Will Give It To You, Because You Deserve It.

Here's The Scripture To Back It Up.

Matthew 6:33-34King James Version (KJV)

33 But seek ye first the kingdom of God, and his righteousness; and all these things shall be added unto you.

34 Take therefore no thought for the morrow: for the morrow shall take thought for the things of itself. Sufficient unto the day is the evil thereof.

When We Honestly Begin To Line Our Lives Up With The Word Of God, We Really Won't Have To Ask God

For Anything. As A Matter Of Fact, All We Need To Do Is Thank Him.

The Bible Says To Be Anxious For Nothing, But In All Thy Ways Acknowledge The Lord...

Here It Is In Scripture, Straight From The Word Of God.

Philippians 4:6-7New King James Version

[6] Be anxious for nothing, but in everything by prayer and supplication, with thanksgiving, let your requests be made known to God; [7] and the peace of God, which surpasses all understanding, will guard your hearts and minds through Christ Jesus.

I Hope That This Book Has Opened Your Eyes And Gave You A Different Outlook On Life And Your Relationship With The Lord.

When My Friend First Started Telling Me To Grab A Hold Of Myself, I Would As He Says, "Buck". It Wasn't Until God Himself Told Me And Started Flooding My Mind With Scriptures That I Had Read And Not Applied. When You Really Commit To Changing, To Walking Upright And Being Obedient To God's Word, You

Won't Continue To Run. You Won't Continue To Make Us Excuses, You'll Be Just Like Me, Available For Change And Your Availability Will Send Out A Spiritual Call And The Heavens Will Answer And Guide You To Becoming Your Best Possible Self With The Word Of God.

It Is As The Kids Say "Crazy"...

Mind Blowing...

AND

A Welcomed Change...

God Will Guide You, Direct You And Navigate You With His Words To Becoming A Better You.

So Enjoy Your Life And More Importantly,

"Grab A Hold Of Yourself" AND Win With God.

2nd Book... Grab A Hold Of Your Spiritual Self

NOTES: Use This Space And Write

Down What You Need To Grab A Hold Of In Your Life
AND
Search Out Scriptures To Back It Up

_____
_____
_____
_____
_____
_____
_____
_____
_____
_____
_____
_____
_____
_____
_____
_____
_____
_____
_____
_____
_____
_____
_____

Thank You
For Purchasing
This Book
I Hope It Helped You

Thank You Again

Pamela Denise Brown

Pamela Denise Brown Books

Focused AND Driven

Published By Books Speak For You Publishing

Specializing In 3, 7 & 21 Day Publishing
Publishing In Over 100 Languages

Printed In The United States

www.Booksspeakforyou.com

BOOKS SPEAK
B
FOR YOU

Pamela Denise Brown, Author

Creator Of Smart Books And Christian Books For Kids

267-318-8933

GRAB A HOLD OF YOURSELF

www.ingramcontent.com/pod-product-compliance
Lightning Source LLC
Chambersburg PA
CBHW051045030426

42339CB00006B/205